Investing in Dividend Stocks for Beginners

How to Invest for Passive Income (Mutual Funds, ETFs, and Index Funds)

By D.K. Livingston

Text Copyright © 2019 D.K. Livingston

All Rights Reserved

No part of this book may be reproduced

in any way without the written

permission of the author.

Disclaimer:

The views expressed within this book are those of the author alone. The information contained within this book is based on the opinions, experiences, and observations of the author and is provided "AS-IS". No warranties of any kind are made. Neither the author nor publisher are engaged in rendering professional services of any kind. Neither the author nor publisher will assume liability or responsibility for any loss or damage related directly or indirectly to the information contained within this book.

The author has attempted to be as accurate as possible with the information contained within this book. Neither the author nor publisher will assume responsibility or liability for any errors, omissions, inconsistencies, or inaccuracies.

Table of Contents

Introduction 1
How Dividends Work 4
ETFs vs Mutual Funds vs Index Funds 6
How to Research Mutual Funds and ETFs 7
How to Select a Broker that is Right for You 8
How to Reduce Risk 14
How to Build a Portfolio 20
How to Find Companies that are Likely to Raise their Dividends ... 24
How to Select Dividend-Paying Stocks 28
Closing 30
More from D.K. Livingston 32

Introduction

Whether an investor is interested in individual stocks or diversified index funds, investing in dividend-paying stocks can be a great way to generate passive income.

While share prices rise and fall, a dividend is guaranteed money that can't be taken away from you.

But knowing which dividend-paying stocks to invest in is crucial. Not all passive income opportunities in the financial markets have the same potential for a return on investment.

Although profits from the dividends can be taken right away and used for other things, reinvesting them in other dividend-paying stocks can improve an investor's portfolio more drastically in the long-term.

In other words, sometimes doing less brings better results.

Many full-time traders and investors often take partial profits, and then they leave the rest of the profits in their investment. This allows the investors to reduce some of the risk, while still staying in the game.

But oftentimes, leaving the investment alone can produce more profits than constantly shifting money around in and out of trades.

Generally, dividends are paid out on a quarterly basis (every three months).

Since dividends are essentially guaranteed income, many people tend to invest in securities that pay dividends, especially during financially uncertain times.

Since many investors tend to move their capital into securities that have the guaranteed income of dividends, that can often cause the price of shares to increase, which of course, can generate even more profits for the traders that plan to eventually sell for capital gains.

When news gets released about a company raising it's dividend payout, this can serve as a catalyst, which can cause many investors to buy shares and move the price up higher.

Dividends can be powerful.

Even if you are working full-time at a high-paying job that you are passionate about, it's still important to know how to have your money work for you.

Unexpected situations can arise, such as:

- Injuries

- Illnesses

- Surgery

- Company cutbacks that lead to a reduction in your salary

- Company cutbacks that lead to the loss of your job

- A devastating turn for the worse in management that make working conditions nearly unbearable

- New coworkers that make things extremely difficult for you

Additionally, learning about dividend investing can be a great way to plan for retirement, because social security benefits might not be quite enough to live off of for as long as a person hopes for.

Aside from research, there is not much more work involved.

Although investing in real estate can often involve hiring carpenters, electricians, and paying for ads to fix up a house and sell it, individual stocks and index funds can feel like much less of a hassle when it comes to generating passive income.

After some research is completed, a BUY button is selected inside a brokerage account, and then the security is purchased.

But how does an investor perform effective research?

How can an investor build and manage a portfolio?

How does an investor know how to reduce risk?

This book is intended to educate you on the fundamentals of investing in dividend-producing investments, focusing primarily on mutual funds, as well as provide you with some insight that can be utilized to become a successful investor.

It will cover:

- **How dividends work**

- **How to research mutual funds and ETFs**

- **How to select a broker that is right for you**

- **How to reduce risk**

- **How to build a portfolio**

- **How to find companies that are likely to raise their dividends**

- **and more**

How Dividends Work

Usually, dividends are paid out on a "per share" basis every quarter, so if a company pays a dollar per share, a person with a hundred shares will generate $100 in dividend income every three months.

It is considered a cash payment that is made possible by the company's earnings, and it's a good way for an investor to make money from a company by investing in it, without having to sell the shares that he or she owns.

A dividend allows the investor to make money from the company without the investor having to give up his or her stake in it.

The only other way to make money from the ownership of a stock without having to sell it is through the use of options strategies.

The managers of a company have to choose what they are going to do with their profits.

They can either choose to reinvest the profits back into their company directly, or they can issue the profits to the investors.

What they decide to do will depend largely on where they stand as a company.

If they feel that share prices will probably not move as high as they did in the past, they might decide to issue "rewards" (dividends) to the shareholders as an incentive to keep them around.

In most cases, when a company is growing at a rapid pace, they won't see much need to offer dividends to shareholders. They might assume that their rapid growth is enough of an incentive to get people to invest in them.

But just because a company offers a dividend, it doesn't necessarily mean that it is no longer growing at a rapid pace.

When a company decides that their days of high-speed growth are behind them, it is likely just a guess.

Personally, I have traded a stock multiple times from a company whose share prices have still been climbing drastically. They offer a dividend, and yet their company seems to be showing no signs of slowing down anytime soon.

The dividend payout is determined by the company's board of directors, who decide how much money gets distributed to the shareholders and how much gets placed back into the company.

Although it seldom happens, sometimes a company will stop issuing dividend payments. It's their right to do so whenever they want.

To give yourself a better chance of not having a company discontinue dividend payments, look for a company that has a long record of issuing them consistently.

Of course, when selecting a dividend-paying company to invest in, it's important to also pay attention to the price performance of the company's shares.

A generous-sounding dividend will not make up for a rapidly declining stock if you plan on selling your shares for profit in the near future.

ETFs vs Mutual Funds vs Index Funds

Since there are so many different things to invest in, it can certainly help to clarify the difference between them.

This chapter will focus on ETFs, mutual funds, and index funds.

ETFs- Exchange-traded funds are bundles of securities that can be traded on an open exchange. Generally, taxation costs and management fees are lower in comparison to those of mutual funds. They can be traded more easily, which allows many investors to view them as more flexible than mutual funds. Pricing information for buys and sells can be obtained in real time. Investors in ETFs are responsible for paying brokerage commissions, management fees, annual fees, as well as other expenses.

Index funds- These funds are not what people invest in directly, as they only act as a mirror for mutual funds. They are a representation of a segment of the market. They can be invested in on an indirect basis through the use of a mutual fund.

Mutual fund- This is a company that gathers money from a large group of investors and invests it in securities. People who invest in mutual funds buy and sell their shares to and from the mutual funds themselves. Investors in mutual funds are responsible for paying sales charges, management fees, annual fees, as well as other expenses. There may also be price uncertainty for an investor of mutual funds because the price at which the investor buys or sells shares might not be calculated until well after the order for the trade has taken place.

If the mutual fund or ETF is based on a 401K or IRA, taxes won't have to be paid until you withdraw money from it.

How to Research Mutual Funds and ETFs

Before investing, you can perform research on a mutual fund of ETF by looking over its prospectus. Reading the prospectus can help you identify the investment strategy and potential risks of the mutual fund or ETF.

The prospectus can be found on the mutual fund's or ETF's website. You can also visit sec.gov/edgar

and download the documents at no charge.

Another option is to call the SEC at their toll-free help line: (800) 732- 0330.

How to Select a Broker that is Right for You

Since different online brokerages have different pros and cons, it's important to choose one that is right for your particular situation.

This chapter will cover some of the most popular online brokers, as well as the pros and cons to each one, how much money they charge per trade via commissions, and what the minimum account balance must be.

Note: Brokers can change their rule structure at anytime, so it's important to visit their websites to verify that the information is current.

E*TRADE

This broker is among the most popular. It was founded in 1982, and their first online trade took place in 1983. They are headquartered in New York City with 30 retail branches across the United States.

Commission fees per trade: $6.95, but only $4.95 with 30 or more trades per quarter

Commission fees for mutual funds: $19.99

Account minimum: $500

Pros

• The platform is known to be beginner-friendly and easy to use

• Offers personalized support and guidance

- Offers independent analyst research

- Has investing tools

- Reduced commission fees for traders who place more than 30 trades per quarter

- Their mobile app makes them more accessible

- Stocks, bonds, options, ETFs, and mutual funds are all available as investment choices

Cons

- There are other brokers that offer smaller commission fees

- There are other brokers that do not require a minimum account balance

Ally

Ally Invest seems to offer a good balance between beginner-friendly and advanced. It's good for beginner investors because there is no minimum account balance required to get started, while the more advanced investor might appreciate their charting, data, and analytical tools.

There are no inactivity fees if the account remains dormant for a while.

Commission fees per trade: $4.95, but only $3.95 with 30 or more trades per quarter

Commission fees for mutual funds: $9.95

Account minimum: $0

Pros

- Lower commission fees than many other brokers

- No minimum account balance requirement

- Customer service is available 24/7

- Tools and informational articles available

- SIPC covered, so up to $250,000 worth of cash funds are protected if *Ally Invest* fails

- Stocks, bonds, options, ETFs, commission-free ETFs, margin accounts, and mutual funds are all available as investment choices

- Offers FOREX trading

- Offers automated portfolio management

Cons

- They do not offer zero-fee transaction for mutual funds

Merrill Edge

Bank of America is their parent company.

Commission fees per trade: $6.95

Account minimum: $0

Pros

• No minimum account balance required

• Customer service available 24/7

• Access to award-winning research

• Has tools that help you make more informed investment decisions

• Stocks, bonds, options, ETFs, mutual funds or professionally managed portfolios are all available as investment choices

• Offers *Market Pro* for active investors

Cons

• There are other brokers that offer cheaper commission fees.

• To qualify for ten $0 online stock and ETF trades per month (the most basic tier), a three-month average balance of at least $20,000 between Bank of America and Merrill Edge accounts must be maintained, which many people might find unrealistic.

AMERITRADE

This brokerage has over 360 branches in the United States.

Commission fees per trade: $6.95

Account minimum: $0

Pros

- No minimum account balance required

- Includes many advanced features

- Investment selection includes equities, options, futures, and FOREX

- Offers personalized coaching via social media, webcasts, and in-person workshops

- Allows the users to "paper trade" for practice without risking real money

- Customer service available 24/7

Cons

- There are other brokers that offer cheaper commission fees.

- Broker-assisted fees are $44.99, which some investors might find expensive.

Fidelity

They used to have an account minimum requirement for mutual funds, but they have now done away with that. They have zero expense ratio for index funds.

Commission fees per trade: $4.95

Account minimum: $0

Pros

- Offers help with planning for retirement and advice on wealth management

- Robust investing tools

- No minimum amount of money required to open an account

- Zero expense ratio index funds

- Zero minimum investment mutual funds

- Customer service available 24/7

- Lower commission fees than many other brokers

- Covered by FDIC and SIPC

Cons

- Need to deposit $50,000-$99,000 to qualify for their promotional offer of 300 free trades over a 2 year period, which some people may find to be too much money.

* * *

If you are feeling indecisive about which online broker to use, know that there is no commitment involved. If you find another broker later on that fits your needs better, you can always switch over.

How to Reduce Risk

Since the financial markets are subject to having ups and downs, it is important to know how to reduce your risk.

One of the best ways to reduce risk as an investor is to diversify.

But it's crucial to know how to diversify.

It makes little sense to buy *Comcast*, *Sprint*, *T-Mobile*, and *Verizon*, and then assume that you have diversified your risk correctly.

That's because all of those stocks belong to the same sector.

When building a portfolio, it's important to include stocks from different sectors to diversify the risk factor.

Each industry will have its own set of catalysts.

If the tech industry is declining significantly, an investor can find relief in the fact that his or her portfolio is still doing well because of the investments that were made in the healthcare industry, energy industry, etc.

Oftentimes, when one industry is down, another one will be up. The investors can then cut their losses with the falling stocks, while continuing to invest in the ones that are doing well.

If the losing stocks are sold early enough, the gains from the well-performing stocks can be larger than the losses from the ones that are not performing well.

Here is a list of the different stock sectors, along with some of the big companies that are in them:

Basic Materials

- Ecolab
- International Paper
- Sherwin-Williams
- Valvoline

Consumer Goods

- Ford
- GM
- Home Depot
- Starbucks
- Target
- Wynn

Consumer Staples

- Costco
- Kraft
- Procter and Gamble
- Walmart

Energy

- BP

- Chevron
- Exon
- Kinder Morgan
- Shell

Financial

- Bank of America
- Goldman Sachs
- JPMorgan
- Morgan Stanley
- Nasdaq
- Wells Fargo
- U.S. Bank

Healthcare

- CVS
- Johnson and Johnson
- Merck
- Medtronic
- Pfizer
- United Healthcare

Industrial

- Boeing

- Caterpillar
- Deere
- Delta
- Honeywell
- Lockheed Martin
- Raytheon
- UPS
- 3M

Real Estate

- Aimco
- AvalonBay Communities
- Simon Property Group

Tech

- Adobe
- Apple
- Facebook
- Google
- IBM
- Intel
- Linkedin
- Mastercard

- Microsoft
- Visa
- Yelp

Telecommunications

- AT&T
- Charter
- Comcast
- Disney
- Sprint
- T-Mobile
- Verizon

Utilities

- Duke Energy
- Public Service Enterprise Group
- NextEra
- NRG
- PG&E
- Xcel

* * *

You don't have to invest in every single one of these sectors to become a successful investor, but diversifying can certainly help reduce risk.

Try to invest in at least four different sectors.

How to Build a Portfolio

When it comes to investing in index funds, building a portfolio can be relatively simple. This is because instead of having to pick out over a dozen different individual stocks, the index fund already includes a group of well-balanced stocks in one index.

The diversification is already built in.

Individual stock selection is often better for short-term investing.

Many individual stocks are known for being more volatile than mutual funds and index funds. They might not offer as much stability as an index fund, but when a stock is on an uptrend, the gains can be larger.

When the uptrend of the volatile individual stock looks like it is coming to an end, the stock can be sold for a profit.

That is why individual stocks can be more work to invest in. They must be monitored often, so the investor can identify trend changes that present possible buy and sell signals.

After the stock is sold, the trader must begin the process all over again; researching the market, studying the charts, and planning the next trade.

Index funds are often better for long-term investing, and they generally require less of a "hands on" approach.

There are individual stocks that pay dividends, and there are index funds that pay dividends. But when building a dividend-producing portfolio, it's important to realize which investment strategy matches your risk-profile.

Determining Where You Want Your Money to Go Based on Risk Tolerance, Age, and Financial Goals

When building a portfolio, you need to identify if you want all of your investment money in a mutual fund, or part of it in a mutual fund with the rest of it in individual stocks.

Before you make that decision, it's important to know what type of investor you are.

- Do you see yourself as more of a short-term trader?

- Do you see yourself as more of a long-term investor?

- Do you enjoy taking an active approach to your investments?

- Do you like to "set it and forget it?"

- Do you see trading as sort of an entertaining "video game" that involves money?

- Do you see trading and investing as overly tedious and time consuming?

- Are you willing to lose big in order to win big?

- Are you willing to put a very large amount of money into an investment, just so it can generate a five percent return a year?

- What is your age?

- What will give you peace of mind?

It can take a long time to gain the experience that is necessary to actively trade stocks. If inexperienced investors get impatient and try to actively trade too soon, they will likely lose a large part of their investments. Their money would be better off in a mutual fund.

Typically, the younger the investor is, the more aggressive he or she can be.

A young person losing ten percent of $2,000 isn't as bad as a sixty-year old losing ten percent of $200,000.

Not only is ten percent of $2,000 less significantly less than ten percent of $200,000, but the younger person also has the added advantage of time.

A thirty-year old still has decades to save for retirement. But a sixty-year old might only have several more years to save for retirement, and therefore, less time to make up for the losses.

Looking at Market Capitalization

Market caps are something to take into consideration when you are assessing your risk tolerance.

Small-cap stocks are known to be more volatile the large-cap stocks. This is largely because there is not enough liquidity in small cap stocks to keep them stable. They are often high risk/high reward.

It might only take a million dollars worth of buying or selling power to shift the price of shares for a small-cap stock significantly.

But it would take tens (or hundreds) of millions of dollars to do the same with a large cap stock. Large-cap stocks are typically low risk/low reward.

There are also mid-cap stocks, which could provide a balance for those that are not interested in high risk/high reward or low risk/low reward scenarios.

If you are assessing individual stocks, make sure their market caps match your risk profile.

Calculating the market capitalization is simple:

Number of outstanding shares multiplied by the current market price of one share.

When a mutual fund is categorized by market capitalization, it is referring to the size of the companies that the fund is invested in, not the size of the mutual fund itself.

Small cap- typically less than $2 billion.

Mid-cap- typically $2 billion to $10 billion.

Large cap- typically $10 billion or more.

Dividend Growth Funds

These are diversified funds that allow you to invest in a low-cost ETF. It is essentially a dividend portfolio that has already been put together.

This type of investing is very passive since it is either actively managed by someone else or it simply tracks an index.

Here a some examples of Dividend Growth Funds:

• ishares International Dividend Growth ETF (IGRO)

• ishares Core Dividend Growth ETF (DGRO)

• PowerShares Dividend Achievers Portfolio ETF (PFM)

• PowerShares S&P 500 High Dividend Low Volatility ETF (SPHD)

• SPDR S&P Dividend ETF (SDY)

How to Find Companies that are Likely to Raise their Dividends

Looking at history can help forecast what is likely to happen in the future. When selecting companies to invest in, it can be beneficial to find ones that have a long history of raising their dividend payouts.

If these companies have a long history of raising their dividend, that makes it more likely that they will continue to do so in the future.

Looking over the *S&P Dividend Aristocrats* list will show you companies that have increased their dividends steadily over the years.

S&P Dividend Aristocrats List

- 3M (MMM)
- Abbott Laboratories (ABT)
- AbbVie Inc (ABBV)
- Aflac (AFL)
- Air Products & Chemicals
- A.O. Smith (AOS)
- Archer-Daniels Midland (ADM)
- AT&T (T)

- Automatic Data (ADP)
- Becton Dickinson (BDX)
- Brown-Forman (BF-B)
- Cardinal Health (CAH)
- Caterpillar Inc. (CAT)
- Chevron (CVX)
- Chubb Ltd (CB)
- Cincinnati Fin. (CINF)
- Cintas (CTAS)
- Clorox (CLX)
- Coca-Cola (KO)
- Colgate-Palmolive (CL)
- Consolidated Edison (ED)
- Dover (DOV)
- Emerson Electric (EMR)
- Ecolab (ECL)
- Exxon Mobil (XOM)
- Federal Realty Inv. Trust
- Franklin Resources (BEN)
- General Dynamics (GD)
- Genuine Parts (GPC)

- Hormel Foods (HRL)
- Illinois Tool Works (ITW)
- Johnson & Johnson (JNJ)
- Kimberly-Clark (KMB)
- Leggett & Platt (LEG)
- Linde PLC (LIN)
- Lowe's Companies (LOW)
- McCormick & Co. (MKC)
- McDonald's (MCD)
- Medtronic (MDT)
- Nucor (NUE)
- Pentair (PNR)
- People's United Financial (PBCT)
- PepsiCo (PEP)
- PPG Industries (PPG)
- Procter & Gamble (PG)
- Roper Technologies Inc. (ROP)
- Sherwin-Williams (SHW)
- S&P Global Inc. (SPGI)
- Stanley Black & Decker (SWK)
- Sysco (SYY)

- Target (TGT)
- T.Rowe Price (TROW)
- VF (VFC)
- Walgreens Boots (WBA)
- Wal-Mart Stores (WMT)
- W.W. Grainger (GWW)

If you are looking for an ETF that tracks the *S&P 500 Dividend Aristocrats Index*, look into *The ProShares S&P 500 Dividend Aristocrats ETF* (NOBL).

How to Select Dividend-Paying Stocks

If you go to [trading view](#) or another charting platform and look up some of the high-dividend-paying companies, you will probably notice a common pattern among them.

The pattern is that the companies with the highest-paying dividends are usually the ones that have been on a long-term downward trend as far as share prices.

As stated in the introduction chapter, a company may offer a dividend when their growth is slowing down in order to keep investors interested, although that's not always the case.

A high dividend might also mean that not enough money is going back into the company.

When selecting dividend-paying stocks, it's NOT a good idea to simply go after the ones that offer the highest-paying dividends.

Realistically, try to look for a company that offers a 3 to 7 percent dividend payment annually. Companies that offer this percentage are more likely to still be growing.

If you see a company with a very high dividend payout, make sure you check the technical charts to see how they have been doing as a company in the long-term.

If investors only look at the dividends, they might end up paying more money than what the dividends are worth.

For an updated list of dividend stocks, visit: https://www.nasdaq.com/dividend-stocks/

Closing

In many cases, the higher the dividend payout, the lower the return will be as far as price per share when it comes time to sell.

The market is always changing, and it takes a fair amount of research to find a good balance of securities that will maximize profits in the long-term.

Be realistic about your expectations, and don't put all of your investment money into something just for the sake of having it produce dividends.

Non-dividend stocks should not be ignored, as many of them have high potential for good returns.

Dividend stocks should only make up a portion of your entire investment portfolio.

A good way to reduce risk is through diversification, and to diversify effectively, an investor should not limit him/herself to dividend stocks.

Buying low-cost index funds can be a very good way to outperform the investors who are constantly chasing trends.

When selecting dividend stocks, look for companies that are still growing.

Reinvesting the income generated through dividends can certainly add up to good profits over time.

More from D.K. Livingston

How to Read Stock Charts, available at all *Amazon* stores, including U.S.

www.ingramcontent.com/pod-product-compliance
Lightning Source LLC
Chambersburg PA
CBHW030739180526
45157CB00008BA/3236

www.ingramcontent.com/pod-product-compliance
Lightning Source LLC
Chambersburg PA
CBHW030739180526
45157CB00008BA/3236